Learning, Rare Disasters, and Asset Prices

1 Introduction

Why are stock returns so high and volatile in many countries? This is a classic question in both economics and finance. In this paper, we provide an answer to this question using a consumption-based asset pricing model in which agents learn about rare disasters that affect their consumption stream.

Following the influential work by Rietz (1988) and Barro (2006), we define a rare disaster as an infrequent large shock that has long-lasting negative effects on aggregate consumption. Examples of a disaster include the Great Depression and World War II. Anecdotal evidence shows that much more often than an actual disaster occurring is that individuals fear that the economy might be headed toward a disaster. During the 2007-2009 financial crisis, many commentators, including Nobel Prize-winning macroeconomists, highlighted the possibility that the U.S. economy could fall into another Great Depression. The markets responded with a large decline in stock prices and increased volatility. The nuclear accident in Japan in early 2011 is another example. This event was followed by a 22% decrease in the Japanese stock market within two days as the country wondered whether the nuclear meltdown could be contained.

To account for the effect of fear on stock markets, we develop a model in which agents have imperfect information regarding the potential realization of a disaster, and they learn by observing their consumption stream. We show that agents' learning endogenously generates time variation in stock returns. Therefore, unlike the existing literature, our learning model explains the level and volatility of stock returns in the U.S. data without relying on realizations of disasters or exogenous variation in the probability of a disaster.

In contrast to some of the earlier disaster literature which assumes that the entire damage of a disaster occurs in a single period,[1] we model disasters based on the empirical results of Nakamura, Steinsson, Barro, and Ursua (2013): a disaster takes multiple periods to unfold, and in turn, causes a persistent decline in consumption. Because the damage of a disaster takes time to unfold, the

---

[1] The assumption that the entire damage of a disaster occurs in a single period is made by many papers on rare disaster models (Rietz (1988); Barro (2006); Farhi and Gabaix (2008); Guo (2009); Gabaix (2012); Wachter (2013)) but is also criticized by others as unrealistic, see for examples, Constantinides (2008), Julliard and Ghosh (2012).

decline in consumption at the onset of a disaster could be confused with a temporary shock in normal time. The estimated posterior probability of one economy experiencing a disaster varies substantially over time, as illustrated in Figure 4 of Nakamura, Steinsson, Barro, and Ursua (2013). In addition, Nakamura, Steinsson, Barro, and Ursua (2013) show that the estimated standard deviations of the short- and long-term shocks during disasters are large, revealing that there is a great amount of uncertainty about the short- and long-term effects of disasters. Therefore, we relax the assumption that agents have perfect information about disasters and allow them to learn about two aspects of rare disasters: (1) whether a decline in consumption is caused by a rare disaster or by a negative transitory shock and (2) the long-term damage of a particular disaster on aggregate consumption. In other words, we assume that the disaster state is unobservable and that the parameters governing the severity of rare disasters are unknown to agents. Agents observe real-time consumption data and update their beliefs regarding the occurrence and the severity of a disaster over time. When agents price assets, they are rational in the sense that they account not only for the uncertainty associated with the occurrence and severity of a disaster but also for future updates of their beliefs concerning this uncertainty.

In our model, learning implies endogenously time-varying stock returns because the updating of agents' beliefs generates time variations in their perceptions of the likelihood and severity of disaster realization. Because of agents' imperfect information about the disaster state, they could assign a relatively high probability to the economy being at the onset of a rare disaster even if the shock to consumption is actually temporary. When the severity of a disaster is uncertain, it becomes more difficult for agents to distinguish a temporary shock from a persistent shock, which causes their beliefs about being in a disaster to become more responsive to temporary shocks to consumption. Furthermore, the updating of agents' beliefs regarding the severity of a disaster leads to additional time variations in the perceived disaster risk. Hence, our model endogenously generates volatile stock returns even in the absence of any disaster realization, a feature that distinguishes our model from the existing literature on rare disasters.

To highlight this feature of our model, we compute asset returns using consumption data simulated from the estimated consumption process by Nakamura, Steinsson, Barro, and Ursua (2013) but with all disaster shocks set to zero. Our model yields an equity premium that matches the observed one using U.S. return data from 1948 to 2008, a period during which the U.S. economy did not experience any disaster. More importantly, the volatility of model-implied stock returns is 17.3%, accounting for 93.5% of the observed volatility. Our model also yields sizable variation in risk-free rates that matches the data. Beyond matching basic asset price moments, our model-based predictive regression of future excess returns on the dividend price ratio generates results that are largely consistent with the data.

In this paper, we highlight the importance of assuming rational agents in asset pricing by presenting the results of our model in parallel with the results of an adaptive learning model. The adaptive learning model shares all elements with our model, except that agents are assumed to ignore future updates of their beliefs when pricing assets.[2] By comparing these two sets of results, we show that the assumption of rational agents is crucial for the time-varying uncertainty regarding rare disasters to generate reasonable movements in asset prices.

This paper is related to two strands of literature. The first strand is the rapidly growing literature on disaster risk following the seminal papers by Rietz (1988) and Barro (2006). This literature studies the effect of rare disasters on asset markets and business cycles (e.g. Liu, Pan, and Wang (2005), Farhi and Gabaix (2008); Gabaix (2012); Gourio (2008a); Gourio (2008b); Wachter (2013); Backus, Chernov, and Martin (forthcoming); Barro and Ursua (2009); Bates (2009); Bollerslev and Todorov (2011); Santa-Clara and Yan (2010); Gourio (2012); Farhi, Fraiberger, Gabaix, Ranciere, and Verdelhan (2009); and Gourio, Siemer, and Verdelhan (2013)). The existing work has proven that the potential risk of disaster occurrence is a powerful mechanism for generating a high risk premium. However, reproducing the dynamics of the risk premium in the data requires time variation in either the quantity or the price of risk because a constant disaster risk produces the risk premium but not its time variation. Thus far, most papers on disaster risk generate a time-varying risk premium by assuming an exogenous process for the probability of a disaster, as in Wachter

---

[2]This is a common assumption in the literature to simplify computation. It is frequently referred to as the anticipated utility approach; see Kreps (1998), Cogley and Sargent (2008), Piazzesi and Schneider (2010), and Johannes, Lochstoer, and Mou (forthcoming).

(2013), Gabaix (2012), Gourio (2012) and Gourio, Siemer, and Verdelhan (2013). However, these papers do not explain the fundamental driving force behind the time-varying disaster probability. In this paper, we use agents' learning to endogenously generate time variation in the perceived risk of a disaster and, in turn, in both dividend-price ratios and equity returns. In this sense, our model provides a foundation for understanding why disaster probability can be assumed to be time varying.[3] Furthermore, our approach also contributes to explaining the predictability of excess returns in the data (see also Brandt, Zeng, and Zhang (2004) and Cogley and Sargent (2008)).

The other strand of literature related to this paper is the literature on learning and asset pricing. Introducing learning into models of asset pricing has been remarkably successful in fitting the persistence and volatility of asset returns, compared with rational expectation models. Two primary sources of uncertainty are generally used to motivate learning: 1) some parameters of the economic model are unknown to agents, and 2) a state—typically a regime or a permanent component of a shock—is not directly observable to agents. It is typical for a learning model to employ only one source of uncertainty. Parameter uncertainty is shown to be important in explaining stock returns (e.g. Timmermann (1996); Timmermann (2001); Weitzman (2007); and Collin-Dufresne, Johannes, and Lochstoer (2013)). State uncertainty, through learning, motivates and disciplines time-varying risk premium (e.g. Veronesi (1999); Veronesi (2004); Brandt, Zeng, and Zhang (2004); Chen and Pakos (2007); and Ghosh and Constantinides (2010)). This paper contributes to this literature by considering an asset pricing model with learning that contains both state uncertainty (disaster realization) and parameter uncertainty (disaster severity).[4] We show that the presence and interaction of these two sources of uncertainty have important implications for asset price dynamics. A related study by Johannes, Lochstoer, and Mou (forthcoming) finds strong evidence that parameter and state learning are important for asset prices. In Johannes,

---

[3]The literature on asset pricing has proposed at least two main classes of rational expectation models to endogenously generate a time-varying equity risk premium. One class of models includes habit formation models represented by Campbell and Cochrane (1999). The other class includes long-run risk models represented by Bansal and Yaron (2004). Our paper complements this literature by suggesting that the learning mechanism can be an alternative means of explaining a time-varying risk premium.

[4]One pioneer paper is Lewis (1989), which shows that a simple learning model in the presence of these two sources of uncertainty is capable of explaining the behavior of forecast errors of U.S. dollar–German mark exchange rate in the early 1980s.

Lochstoer, and Mou (forthcoming), both state uncertainty and parameter uncertainty are present, but agents are assumed to ignore parameter uncertainty when pricing assets.

2 The Model

This section presents our benchmark asset pricing model with learning. After introducing the consumption process, we explain how agents update their beliefs and how the belief-updating affects asset prices.

2.1 Consumption process with rare disasters

We adopt the following process for consumption growth in which disasters affect long-run consumption:

$$c_t \equiv \Delta \log C_t = \mu + I_t \theta_\tau + \eta_t. \tag{2.1}$$

In this expression, c_t denotes the consumption growth at time t, C_t is the aggregate consumption at time t, and Δ denotes a first difference. In the normal state, the mean growth rate is μ and the shock to consumption growth is η_t, which is i.i.d. normally distributed with mean zero and variance σ_η^2. The disaster term in this consumption process consists of two parts: the disaster indicator I_t and the severity of the disaster θ_τ. I_t takes two values (0 or 1) and follows a Markov chain with transition matrix Q, where $\sum_j Q_{ij} = 1$, $i, j = 0, 1$. $I_t = 0$ indicates a normal state and $I_t = 1$ is a disaster state. When a disaster occurs, due to the persistence build into the transition matrix, the disaster generally lasts for several periods and we call the consecutive periods with $I_t = 1$ a "disaster episode." In the disaster episode, the mean consumption growth is shifted by θ_τ. We assume that at the beginning of each disaster episode, θ_τ is drawn randomly from a normal distribution $F(\theta)$, with mean μ_θ and variance σ_θ^2, and stays constant until after the disaster. Thus, θ_τ is a disaster-specific parameter with its subscript τ standing for a particular disaster episode.

The specification in equation (2.1) is meant to capture two features of a disaster suggested by Nakamura, Steinsson, Barro, and Ursua (2013): 1) a disaster typically lasts for several periods;

and 2) each disaster is unique in terms of its long-term damage. Our specification is a simplified version of the empirical model by Nakamura, Steinsson, Barro, and Ursua (2013), and we rely on their estimates to calibrate the consumption process. We abstract from a short-term effect of a disaster for the sake of simplicity and we discuss briefly in the conclusion the implications of adding back the short-term effect in our model. Note that except for the time-varying drift in the consumption process, this specification is shared by many other models in the asset-pricing literature since the regime-switching property of the consumption growth is commonly regarded as important for understanding consumption-based asset pricing (e.g., Cecchetti et al. 1990, 1993, 2000; Kandel and Stambaugh 1991; Miao and Ju 2011).

2.2 Bayesian learning

Agents in the benchmark model observe current and past realizations of consumption $c^t \equiv \{c_s\}_{s=0}^{t}$ but do not observe current and past states $\{I_s\}_{s=0}^{t}$ or disaster-specific parameters $\{\theta_s\}_{s=0}^{\tau}$. The uncertainty about the unobservable state is referred to as *state uncertainty* and the uncertainty about the unobservable parameter is referred to as *parameter uncertainty*. In this subsection, we explain how agents update their beliefs when they have to learn the state I_t and the disaster-specific parameter θ_τ at the same time.

The presence of the two sources of uncertainty distinguishes our model from the existing literature on learning, where agents typically have perfect information about either the state or the parameter. If I_t can be observed and the uncertainty is only about θ_τ, our model fits into the familiar framework of econometric learning.[5] If, instead, the disaster-specific parameter θ_τ is observable and the uncertainty is only about I_t, our model reduces to a standard hidden Markov regime-switching model.

---

[5]The term "econometric learning" is taken from Evans and Honkapohia (2001). It refers to the approach that puts economic agents in the shoes of statisticians or econometricians whose knowledge about the parameters of the model comes from past observable data.

2.2.1 Learning trigger - definition

Each time a disaster starts, parameter θ_τ is drawn from $F(\theta)$ and remains constant until after the disaster. This assumption of our model is different from a standard one in the literature on parameter uncertainty. In a standard model of econometric learning, the unknown parameters are constant over time, and agents should use all past data to form their beliefs. In our benchmark model, parameter θ_τ that governs the severity of a disaster is constant only over one disaster episode and is independent of all previous disasters. Therefore, it is optimal for agents to update their beliefs about θ_τ only when a disaster starts if they know the disaster state, I_t. However, agents in our model do not directly observe the disaster state, I_t, so we assume that they perform a statistical test each period of whether the economy is in a disaster state in order to decide when to start updating their beliefs about the severity of the disaster, θ_τ.[6] The result of this statistical test is represented by the learning trigger as defined below.

Definition. *The learning trigger, S_t, is an indicator that can take two values: **off** or **on**. When the learning trigger is **off** at the end of period t, agents ignore the small probability of an ongoing disaster and assume that $I_t = 0$. When the learning trigger is **on** at the end of period t, agents entertain the possibility of being in a disaster episode and update their beliefs about parameter θ_τ that is specific to this disaster.*

The basic intuition for the "learning trigger" is that agents are not always suspicious that there is a disaster unless they observe some evidence of it. Although in theory a Bayesian learner in our model should always consider the possibility that there is a disaster with some probability, we find it more reasonable to assume that agents will not take a booming economy as a sign for a disaster even with a small probability. The learning trigger is set up such that agents in our model will investigate the severity of a disaster only when there is a significant chance that the

---

[6]See Kasa and Cho (2011) for another example of learning along this line. Economically, one could argue in favor of the learning trigger that in a world where learning is costly for agents, agents would only engage in learning activity if there is sufficient benefit to do so. Technically, introducing a learning trigger keeps the model tractable since the state space would otherwise grow over time to be infinite-dimensional. In our model, the disaster state, I_t, is not directly observable to agents. Thus, without a learning trigger, agents in each period t face the uncertainty that a new disaster may have started in period $t, t-1, t-2, \ldots$. This would lead to an infinite number of beliefs about θ_τ and render the model intractable.

current consumption data are generated by shocks beyond the one in normal time. The real-world counterpart of the abnormal data is an event that marks the start of a turmoil. Examples include Black Tuesday in October 1929 as the start of the Great Depression, the collapse of Bear Stearns and Lehman Brothers in the Fall of 2008 as the start of the Great Recession, the Tunisian revolution in December 2010 as the start of the Arab Spring, the earthquake and tsunami in March 2011 as the start of the nuclear crisis in Japan, etc. Given that a period of turmoil usually has a clearly marked start, we grant this knowledge to the agents in our model as well.

2.2.2 Learning trigger - the uniformly most powerful test

Next we discuss the implementation of the learning trigger. The learning trigger takes the form of a statistical test with the null hypothesis being $I_t = 1$ against the alternative hypothesis, $I_t = 0$:

$$H_0 : I_t = 1 \text{ and } H_1 : I_t = 0. \tag{2.2}$$

If we reject the null hypothesis, the learning trigger S_t is set to off; otherwise, it is left on. Denote $S^t \equiv \{S_s\}_{s=0}^t$. Conditional on S^{t-1}, we construct the test statistic, $\lambda(c_t)$, using the data c_t:

$$\begin{aligned}\lambda(c_t) &= \frac{L\left(c_t | H_0, c^{t-1}, S^{t-1}\right)}{L\left(c_t | H_1, c^{t-1}, S^{t-1}\right)} \\ &= \int_\theta \exp\left(\frac{\theta_\tau}{\sigma_\eta^2} c_t - \frac{\theta_\tau^2 + 2\theta_\tau \mu}{2\sigma_\eta^2}\right) \Pr\left(\theta_\tau | c^{t-1}, S^{t-1}\right) d\theta_\tau, \end{aligned} \tag{2.3}$$

where $L(c_t|\cdot)$ is the conditional likelihood function. If $S_{t-1} = on$, $\Pr(\theta_\tau|c^{t-1}, S^{t-1})$ is agents' beliefs about θ_τ inherited from last period; if $S_{t-1} = off$, $\Pr(\theta_\tau|c^{t-1}, S^{t-1})$ is the unconditional density $f(\theta_\tau)$ from the normal distribution $F(\theta)$.

We reject the null hypothesis if the test statistic $\lambda(c_t)$ is below a cutoff ϕ. According to the Neyman-Pearson lemma, this test is a uniformly most powerful test given a size α that is determined by ϕ:

$$\alpha = \Pr\left(\lambda(c_t) < \phi | H_0\right). \tag{2.4}$$

Therefore, using this statistical test, we can control the probability that agents mistakenly reject the null (turn the learning trigger off while there is a disaster) and maximize the probability of turning off the learning trigger in the absence of a disaster.

2.2.3 Learning with the learning trigger

After each realization of c_t, agents' beliefs about state I_t can be updated using the Bayes' rule:

$$\Pr\left(I_t = 1 | S^{t-1}, c^t\right) = \frac{\Pr\left(c_t | S^{t-1}, I_t = 1, c^{t-1}\right) \Pr\left(I_t = 1 | S^{t-1}, c^{t-1}\right)}{\Pr\left(c_t | S^{t-1}, c^{t-1}\right)}, \quad (2.5)$$

where the likelihood function of c_t is obtained by integrating out the unknown parameter θ_τ using its conditional distribution, $\Pr\left(\theta_\tau | S^{t-1}, c^{t-1}\right)$, specified in the previous subsection. The prior belief about the state I_t is:

$$\Pr\left(I_t = 1 | S_{t-1} = off, S^{t-2}, c^{t-1}\right) = Q_{01} \quad (2.6)$$

by the definition of the learning trigger and

$$\Pr\left(I_t = 1 | S_{t-1} = on, S^{t-2}, c^{t-1}\right)$$
$$= Q_{01} \Pr\left(I_{t-1} = 0 | S_{t-1} = on, S^{t-2}, c^{t-1}\right) + Q_{11} \Pr\left(I_{t-1} = 1 | S_{t-1} = on, S^{t-2}, c^{t-1}\right). \quad (2.7)$$

Meanwhile, the value of S_t is determined according to the statistical test described in the previous subsection.

If S_t is on, c_t is used to further update agents' beliefs about the disaster-specific parameter θ_τ:

$$\Pr\left(\theta_\tau | S^{t-1}, c^t\right) = \frac{\Pr\left(c_t | \theta_\tau, I_t = 1\right) \Pr\left(\theta_\tau | S^{t-1}, c^{t-1}\right)}{\Pr\left(c_t | S^{t-1}, I_t = 1, c^{t-1}\right)}. \quad (2.8)$$

In this case, the updated beliefs about both the state and the parameter are recorded using

$$\Pr\left(I_t = 1 | S_t = on, S^{t-1}, c^t\right) \equiv \Pr\left(I_t = 1 | S^{t-1}, c^t\right); \quad (2.9)$$

$$\Pr\left(\theta_\tau | S_t = on, S^{t-1}, c^t\right) \equiv \Pr\left(\theta_\tau | S^{t-1}, c^t\right). \tag{2.10}$$

If S_t is off, however, neither of the beliefs will be recorded as agents assume $I_t = 0$ and the parameter θ_τ of the past disaster is not relevant for future disasters.

2.3 Asset pricing

We study a representative-agent endowment economy with two assets: a risk-free bond and an equity that pays aggregate dividends D_t each period. We use R^f_{t+1} and R^e_{t+1} to denote their gross returns from period t to period $t+1$, respectively. Agents in our model are assumed to have Epstein-Zin preferences (Epstein and Zin (1989)), which are defined recursively as:

$$U_t = \left\{ (1-\beta) C_t^{1-1/\psi} + \beta \left[E_t \left(U_{t+1}^{1-\gamma} \right) \right]^{\frac{1-1/\psi}{1-\gamma}} \right\}^{\frac{1}{1-1/\psi}}, \tag{2.11}$$

where C_t is consumption at period t, U_t is the utility at period t, β is the time discount factor, ψ is the inter-temporal elasticity of substitution (IES), and γ is the coefficient of relative risk aversion. These preferences imply the stochastic discount factor M_{t+1}:

$$M_{t+1} = \beta^\epsilon \left(\frac{C_{t+1}}{C_t} \right)^{-\gamma} \left(\frac{PC_{t+1} + 1}{PC_t} \right)^{\epsilon - 1}, \tag{2.12}$$

where $\epsilon = (1-\gamma)(1-1/\psi)^{-1}$ and PC_t is the price-dividend ratio at period t for an asset that delivers aggregate consumption as its dividend each period. Using this stochastic discount factor, PC_t can be obtained using the following recursion:

$$PC_t = \beta \left\{ E_t \left[\left(\frac{C_{t+1}}{C_t} \right)^{-\gamma+1} (PC_{t+1} + 1)^\epsilon \right] \right\}^{1/\epsilon}. \tag{2.13}$$

We now turn to specifying the dividend process of the equity. It is common in the literature (e.g., Ju and Miao (2012); Johannes, Lochstoer, and Mou (forthcoming)) to model dividends and consumption separately since the aggregate dividend is much more volatile than aggregate consumption in the data. However, to maintain the basic feature of an endowment economy, the mean of the long-run dividend growth is usually adjusted to be equal to that of the long-run levered consumption growth (Bansel and Yaron 2004; Ju and Miao (2012)). We thus follow the literature to model the dividend process as:

$$\frac{D_{t+1}}{D_t} = \left(\frac{C_{t+1}}{C_t}\right)^\lambda exp(g_d + \sigma_d \varepsilon_t). \quad (2.14)$$

where λ is the leverage ratio,[7] g_d helps to match the long-run dividend and consumption growth, $\varepsilon_t \sim N(0,1)$ is the dividend shock, and σ_d is used to match the volatility of dividends in the data. With this dividend process and the stochastic discount factor M_{t+1}, the price-dividend ratio for the equity, denoted by PD_t, can be obtained using

$$PD_t = E_t\left[\beta^\epsilon \left(\frac{C_{t+1}}{C_t}\right)^{-\gamma+\lambda} \left(\frac{PC_{t+1}+1}{PC_t}\right)^{\epsilon-1}(PD_{t+1}+1)\right]\exp\left(g_d + \frac{1}{2}\sigma_d^2\right). \quad (2.15)$$

If agents can observe θ_t and I_t perfectly, both price-dividend ratios PC_t and PD_t are functions of (θ_t, I_t). In our model, however, neither θ_t nor I_t is directly observable, so we have to replace them by the corresponding agents' beliefs, $\Pr(\theta_\tau|S^t, c^t)$ and $\pi_t \equiv \Pr(I_t = 1|S^t, c^t)$. Denote $PD[\Pr(\theta_\tau|S^t, c^t), \pi_t]$ as the price-dividend ratio function (PDR function hereafter) for the equity under imperfect information. It satisfies the following recursion:

$$PD[\Pr(\theta_\tau|S^t, c^t), \pi_t]\exp\left(-g_d - \frac{1}{2}\sigma_d^2\right)$$
$$= \beta^\epsilon E_t\left[\exp[(\lambda-\gamma)c_{t+1}]\left(\frac{PC_{t+1}+1}{PC_t}\right)^{\epsilon-1}[PD[\Pr(\theta_\tau|S^{t+1}, c^{t+1}), \pi_{t+1}]+1]\right], \quad (2.16)$$

where $PC_t = PC[\Pr(\theta_\tau|S^t, c^t), \pi_t]$ and $PC_{t+1} = PC[\Pr(\theta_\tau|S^{t+1}, c^{t+1}), \pi_{t+1}]$ are the PDR functions for the unlevered consumption claim under imperfect information that are obtained using the recursion (2.13).[8]

In addition to replacing (θ_t, I_t) by the beliefs, imperfect information about θ_t and I_t also changes

---

[7] Abel (1999) shows that using the power parameter λ is a convenient way to model leverage. $\lambda = 1$ corresponds to an unlevered equity, and values of λ larger than 1 correspond to levered equities.

[8] In the computation, we replace $\Pr(\theta_\tau|S^t, c^t)$ by its mean and variance since it is a normal distribution.

the expectation operator E_t. In particular, conditional on the information set at period t, the distribution of future $c_{t+1} = \mu + I_{t+1}\theta_\tau + \eta_{t+1}$ is determined by $\Pr(\theta_\tau|S^t, c^t)$ and π_t due to the persistence of θ_τ and I_t. Each future realization of c_{t+1} implies a set of updated state variables, $\Pr(\theta_\tau|S^{t+1}, c^t, c_{t+1})$ and $\Pr(I_{t+1} = 1|S^{t+1}, c^t, c_{t+1})$, which are in turn associated with a particular future PDR. The expectation is taken by averaging across all possible future c_{t+1} and the associated PDRs. A similar methodology applies to the computation of the risk-free rate.

The literature on asset pricing with parameter uncertainty usually assumes that agents are adaptive learners - also called the anticipated utility approach - in the sense that they view parameters as constants when pricing assets, whereas their beliefs about parameters are in fact updated over time (e.g., Kreps (1998); Cogley and Sargent (2008); Piazzesi and Schneider (2010) and Johannes, Lochstoer, and Mou (forthcoming)). The computation of the PDR functions in our model overcomes this inconsistency between asset pricing and learning. To the best of our knowledge, we are the first to treat the belief about the parameter - a distribution - as the state variable in the PDR function under Epstein-Zin preferences. Our model thus takes into account how the time-varying parameter uncertainty affects asset returns.

2.4 Calibration

Table 1 reports the parameter values we use in our simulation exercises. The parameters governing consumption are set equal to their posterior means estimated in Nakamura, Steinsson, Barro, and Ursua (2013) whenever possible. The period in our model is one year to be consistent with the frequency in Nakamura, Steinsson, Barro, and Ursua (2013). Recall that our specification of the consumption process simplifies the empirical model in Nakamura, Steinsson, Barro, and Ursua (2013) by omitting transitory disaster shocks. This simplification does not invalidate the suitability of their estimates to our model since the effect of transitory shocks disappears over the long run. In other words, our agents are endowed with the same knowledge about the long-run consumption growth as the econometricians who study the cross-country consumption data over the last 100 years. In fact, by using this parameter configuration for the consumption process, we

Table 1: Calibration parameters

Parameter	Symbol	Value
Mean of Consumption Growth	μ	0.022
Std. Dev. of Consumption Growth Shock	σ_η	0.018
Mean of Disaster Shock	μ_θ	-0.024
Std. Dev. of Disaster Shock	σ_θ	0.121
Prob. to Enter a Disaster	Q_{01}	0.028
Prob. to Exit a Disaster	Q_{10}	0.165
Leverage Ratio	λ	2.5
Mean Adjustment of Dividend Growth	g_d	-0.0278
Std. Dev. of Dividend Growth Shock	σ_d	0.121
Discount Factor	β	0.977
Risk Aversion	γ	6.5
IES	Ψ	2
Size of Test	α	10%

are putting ourselves in a more challenged position in matching the level and volatility of equity returns because the consumption process in our model, by omitting transitory disaster shocks, is less volatile than the actual consumption data.

The leverage ratio, λ, is set to 2.5, which is a conservative level compared to other models in the literature.[9] As discussed in the previous subsection, g_d in the dividend process (2.14) is picked so that the long-run dividend growth is equal to the long-run consumption growth.[10] Using the parameter values of the consumption process, we thus set g_d to be -0.0278. The standard deviation of the dividend shock, σ_d, is used to match the volatility of dividends in the data, which is 0.129 for our annual sample from 1948 to 2008. We thus find $\sigma_d = 0.121$.

The preference parameters are standard with a rather low risk aversion coefficient of 6.5 and the IES equal to 2.[11] We set the time discount factor, β, equal to 0.977 to roughly match the average risk-free rate in the data.

---

[9]There is no consensus in the literature about the level of leverage. Typically the parameter value ranges from 1.5 to 4 (Nakamura, Steinsson, Barro, and Ursua (2013), Gourio (2012), Bansal and Yaron (2004)).

[10]Note that with our specification of the consumption process, long-run consumption growth takes into account the impact of disasters.

[11]Bansal and Yaron (2004) rely on a risk aversion coefficient of 10, while the model of Mehra and Prescott (1985) requires a risk aversion coefficient of about 40 to match the equity premium. The Campbell and Cochrane (1999) model implies a time-varying local risk aversion coefficient larger than 30 in simulations.

The only free parameter left in our learning model is the size of the test that determines the state of the learning trigger. In the literature on statistical tests, it is common to set the test size to be 10%, 5% or 1%. In our application, a larger size implies a higher probability for agents to mistakenly turn off the learning trigger, which would cause them to learn less frequently. We use a conservative 10% in our calibration so that the results to be presented can be viewed as the lower bound of how much learning can affect asset returns. Reducing the test size can only strengthen the learning effect. The appendix provides robustness check of our results to changes in the size of the test.

3 Results

One novelty of our asset pricing model is the presence of both parameter uncertainty and state uncertainty in agents' learning. To gain a better understanding of how the two sources of uncertainty affect learning and asset prices, we compute and compare asset returns under four model variants.

The first model assumes that agents have perfect information about the current and past states of the economy $(I_s)_{s=0}^{t}$ but they view parameter θ_τ as a new draw from distribution $F(\theta)$ each period. This model shuts down learning and is designed to capture the effect of parameter uncertainty on asset returns. We label this model as "no learning."

The second model is labeled as "state learning" in which agents learn about disaster state I_t conditional on perfect knowledge about θ_τ. This model demonstrates the effect of state uncertainty on asset returns and is one variant of the well-known hidden Markov regime-switching models.

The third model is our "rational learning" (benchmark) model in which agents learn both parameter θ_τ and state I_t at the same time. Parameter uncertainty and state uncertainty interact with each other in this model and the interaction has important implications for asset returns. In addition, we assume that agents are rational learners in the sense that they take into account the future updates of their beliefs about θ_τ when they price assets. In other words, the belief about θ_τ is a state variable in the PDR function, which is computed using the recursion shown in equation

(2.16).

To illustrate the importance of "rational learning" in asset pricing, we add a fourth model, "adaptive learning" model, to mimic a common approach used in the literature.[12] This model shares all elements with the rational learning (benchmark) model except that agents' beliefs about θ_τ are assumed to be fixed when they price assets.

We further group the results into two sets. The first set shows the behavior of equity returns and risk-free rates implied by these four models when there is a disaster. The second set reports quantitative results of asset returns implied by these four models using consumption data that are simulated without any realization of disasters.

3.1 A disaster realization

In this subsection, we investigate the dynamics of asset returns with a sample disaster episode starting at period 5 and lasting for 6 periods (years). The long-term damage on consumption growth of this particular disaster is set to be 4% each period during the disaster, which implies a total 24% drop of consumption in the long run. All other shocks, η_t, are set to zero.

Figure 1 shows the evolution of agents' posterior beliefs that the economy is in a disaster. Panel (a) shows the model with no learning, so the beliefs are equal to zero when $I_t = 0$ and one when $I_t = 1$. In the state learning model shown in Panel (b), agents face only state uncertainty but not parameter uncertainty. As a result, their posterior beliefs that the economy is in a disaster increase rapidly after the disaster starts at period 5, reaching nearly 1 at period 7.

Panel (c) in Figure 1 shows the beliefs in the rational learning (benchmark) model, in which agents face both state uncertainty and parameter uncertainty.[13] Without perfect knowledge about the mean of consumption growth in the disaster state, agents take longer to learn about the true state of the economy. Panel (d) shows the difference in beliefs between the state learning model

---

[12]E.g., Kreps (1998), Cogley and Sargent (2008), Johannes, Lochstoer, and Mou (forthcoming), and Piazzesi and Schneider (2010). It is important to clarify that these authors hold the mean belief constant and do not consider the entire distribution. This modification does not qualitatively change our results.

[13]The dynamics of agents' beliefs in the adaptive learning model are identical to those in the rational learning (benchmark) model because these two models only differ in the computation of returns.

and the rational learning (benchmark) model.

Note that the difference in Panel (d) is first positive and then negative, reflecting the fact that learning about the true state is significantly slowed by the presence of parameter uncertainty. Also note that at the early stage of the disaster when parameter uncertainty is most pronounced, the difference in belief is the largest. As more observations of consumption growth are accumulated over time, parameter uncertainty diminishes and in turn, the difference in beliefs becomes smaller.

Figure 1: A Disaster Realization, Part 1

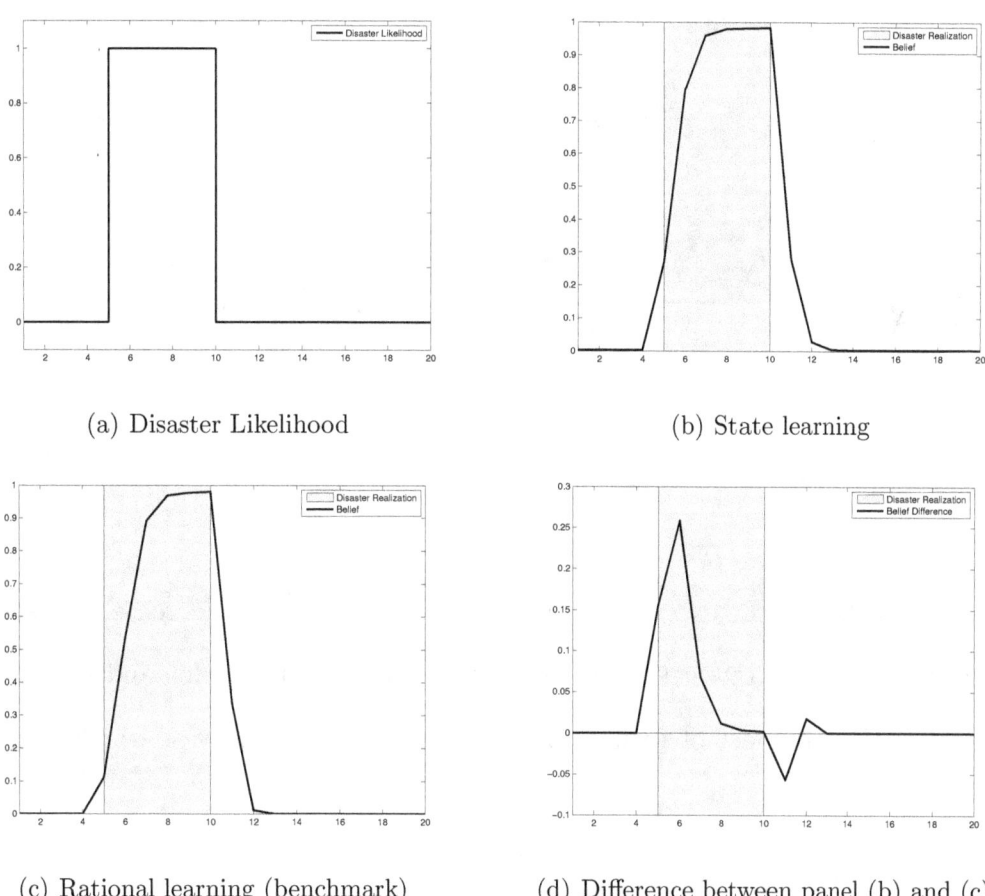

(a) Disaster Likelihood

(b) State learning

(c) Rational learning (benchmark)

(d) Difference between panel (b) and (c)

Figure 2 shows asset returns in the four models. The black solid line is the time series of equity returns and the black dashed line is the time series of risk-free rates. The green line is the de-trended $\log C_t$ path.

Let us first look at the model with no learning in Figure 2, Panel (a). At the onset of a disaster,

Figure 2: A Disaster Realization, Part 2

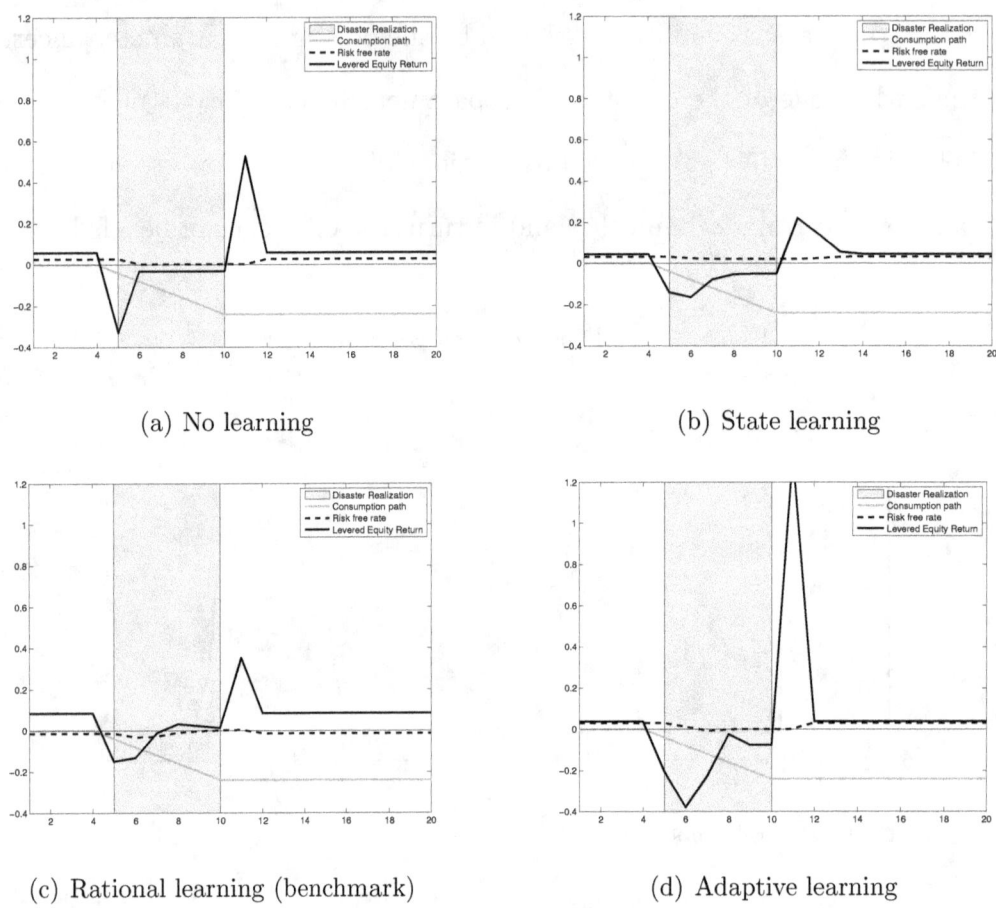

(a) No learning

(b) State learning

(c) Rational learning (benchmark)

(d) Adaptive learning

the stock market crashes as the expected future consumption growth decreases. The risk-free rate barely changes upon impact but it subsequently drops due to higher demand for the safer asset. After the disaster, the prospect of future consumption growth improves, which leads to a stock market boom.

The initial stock market crash at the onset of a disaster and the stock market boom afterwards are common patterns across all models. The magnitude and persistence of the crash and the boom differ across models.

Now we turn to the state learning model shown in Figure 2, Panel (b). Compared to the model with no learning (Figure 2, Panel (a)), both the crash and the boom become more gradual: the movements in equity returns are smaller but more persistent. This change is driven by agents' learning about state I_t. As shown in Panel (b) of Figure 1, at the onset of a disaster, agents' posterior beliefs that the economy is in a disaster are as low as 25%. Due to the presence of state uncertainty at the onset of the disaster, the equity price does not drop as dramatically as in the model with no learning, resulting in a gradual fall of the equity return. After the disaster episode ends at period 10, it takes agents a couple of periods to be sure that the economy has come back to the normal state. The equity price thus rises gradually, as does the equity return.

Finally, let us consider the rational learning (benchmark) model (Figure 2, Panel (c)) and the adaptive learning model (Figure 2, Panel (d)). These two panels differ majorly in the sizes of the stock market crash and boom at the onset and conclusion of the disaster. In particular, the crash and boom are significantly larger in the adaptive learning model.

Recall that the difference between these two models lies solely in how agents price assets. Adaptive agents ignore changes in their future beliefs and only account for their current beliefs about θ_τ in pricing assets. Rational agents, on the other hand, not only acknowledge their imperfect information about θ_τ, but also account for future updates in their beliefs about θ_τ when pricing assets. Therefore, when agents observe a large negative shock on consumption growth and think that θ_τ is likely to be very negative, rational agents realize that their current pessimistic view about the severity of the disaster can be changed in the future, whereas adaptive agents believe that the current disaster is a severe one. Consequently, the equity return in the latter case responds more aggressively to the negative shock in consumption growth, generating a more severe stock market crash. A similar argument can be made for the more substantial boom after the disaster.

It is worth noting that equity returns during a disaster episode are more volatile in the no learning model (Figure 2, Panel (a)) than in the rational learning (benchmark) model (Figure 2, Panel (c)). However, our quantitative results in the next subsection show that using simulated consumption data, the rational learning (benchmark) model generates more volatile equity returns than the no learning model does because in the former case, agents could temporarily confuse a shock in the normal state with a disaster shock. The temporary confusion triggers learning and generates additional time variation in equity returns beyond the no learning model.

3.2 Quantitative results

In this subsection, we compute asset returns implied by our rational learning (benchmark) model and the other three model variants using simulated consumption data. The consumption data are simulated using the data generating process specified in equation (2.1) with no disaster realization throughout (I_t is set to zero at all periods).[14]

The aim of this exercise is to compare moments of the model-implied returns to those of U.S. data from 1948 to 2008. Our return data are annual returns of the U.S. one-month Treasury bill and U.S. major stock indexes (NYSE/AMEX/NASDAQ), obtained from the CRSP database. We use the annualized monthly CPI data from BLS to deflate nominal returns. Arguably, the U.S. economy did not suffer from any macroeconomic disaster during the period from 1948 to 2008.[15] Thus, this exercise highlights the ability of our rational learning (benchmark) model in generating high equity premium and reasonable return variation even without any realization of disasters, a feature that distinguishes our model from many others in the literature on rare disasters.

3.2.1 Moments

Table 2 reports the means and standard deviations of risk-free rates and equity returns, expressed in percentages. R^f denotes the risk-free rate, and R^e denotes the equity return. $E(\cdot)$ is the mean of returns, and $\sigma(\cdot)$ is the standard deviation of returns. Panel I reports moments of the actual data. Panel II reports the corresponding model-implied return moments. We first explain the results of equity returns and then discuss the risk-free rates.

Row 1 in Table 2 reports the results from the no learning model. Recall that agents are assumed to know the current state of the economy perfectly while they are still exposed to the disaster risk for the next period. In addition, the disaster risk incorporates time-invariant parameter uncertainty in the sense that parameter θ_τ is viewed as a random draw from $F(\theta)$ each period. Therefore, the

---

[14]Since there is no disaster realization in the simulation, the disaster parameter θ_τ is never drawn. Therefore, in computing the case of state learning, we assume that agents think the true θ_τ is at its prior mean value. Each simulated consumption path has 60 periods like our data and we repeat the simulation 10,000 times to take the averages of asset return moments across simulations.

[15]The posterior probability that the U.S. economy was in a disaster is nearly zero from 1948 to 2008 according to Figure 4 in Nakamura, Steinsson, Barro, and Ursua (2013).

Table 2: Asset pricing moments

Moments	$E(R^f)$	$\sigma(R^f)$	$E(R^e)$	$\sigma(R^e)$	$E(R^e) - E(R^f)$
			Panel I: Data		
U.S. data from 1948 to 2008	1.14	2.35	8.54	18.50	7.40
			Panel II: Models		
1. No learning	2.79	0.00	6.55	13.69	3.75
2. State learning	3.05	0.22	5.37	14.66	2.32
3. Rational learning (benchmark)	1.25	2.17	9.29	17.31	8.05
4. Adaptive learning	3.19	0.29	10.25	46.52	7.05

The data are computed using annual returns of the U.S. one-month Treasury-bill and U.S. major stock indexes (NYSE/AMEX/NASDAQ) from 1948 to 2009, obtained from CRSP. All nominal returns are deflated using the annualized monthly CPI data from BLS.

equity premium in this model reflects the price of the disaster risk with parameter uncertainty.[16] However, without any realization of disasters throughout the simulated consumption path, the time-invariant state and the time-invariant parameter uncertainty imply that the PDR of the equity remains constant. As a result, all the variation in equity returns comes from shocks to the dividend process ($\sigma_d \varepsilon_t$).

Row 2 in Table 2 shows the results from the state learning model. Compared to the no learning model, the volatility of equity returns is larger due to the time-varying state uncertainty. However, because the state learning model assumes away parameter uncertainty, the equity premium is lower than its counterpart in the no learning model. This result reveals that a standard hidden Markov regime-switching model typically requires either high risk-aversion or a large mean shift in consumption growth to match excess equity returns.

---

[16] In this sense, the no learning model resembles the model used in Nakamura, Steinsson, Barro, and Ursua (2013).

Rows 3 and 4 in Table 2 show the rational learning (benchmark) model and the adaptive learning model, respectively. Recall that both parameter uncertainty and state uncertainty are present in these two models. As a result, the equity premium and the volatility of equity returns are higher than their counterparts in the no learning model and the state learning model. Compared to the rational learning (benchmark) model, the model with adaptive agents yields lower equity returns and a significantly higher equity return volatility. Borrowing the intuition obtained in Section 3.1 on the return dynamics during a disaster episode, we can understand that the higher return volatility in the adaptive learning model stems from ignoring agents' belief-updating in asset pricing. Since adaptive agents view their current beliefs about parameter θ_τ as lasting indefinitely, the equity price responds more aggressively to changes in the current beliefs than it does when agents are rational and understand that their future beliefs about parameter θ_τ will be updated with new consumption data.

To understand why the equity returns are higher with rational agents, it is worthwhile to note that the posterior means of agents' beliefs about parameter θ_τ are higher than its unconditional mean most of the time when the consumption data are simulated without any realization of disasters. Adaptive agents price assets with the beliefs that the current disaster is mild, whereas rational agents are aware that there might be worse news coming and the disaster could be worse than currently known. Therefore, a higher risk is priced into the equity when agents are rational and in turn the equity yields higher returns.

We now compare the risk-free rates across various models. A notable feature of our rational learning (benchmark) model is that it implies much lower and more volatile risk-free rates than the other three models. Once again, this feature can be attributed to the fact that rational agents take into account their belief-updating in the future when they price assets. As discussed before, an awareness of future changes in the posterior mean of beliefs about θ_τ implies a higher risk in future consumption. The higher risk not only generates higher equity returns but also increases the demand for the risk-free asset and lowers the risk-free returns. Furthermore, this risk varies with how long agents have been actively learning. The longer the learning trigger is activated (i.e.,

$S_t = on$), the less parameter uncertainty is present due to the accumulated consumption data. When agents are more confident about their estimate of θ_τ, the posterior mean of their future beliefs about θ_τ will be less sensitive to new data, which reduces agents' perceived risk in future consumption stemming from their future belief-updating. This mechanism creates an additional time dependence of risk-free rates and is only at work when agents are rational and face both state uncertainty and parameter uncertainty. As a result, risk-free rates are much more volatile in our rational learning (benchmark) model.

Note that the U.S. data also feature low and relatively volatile risk-free rates. Although we pick the value of the time discount factor β to match the first moment of risk-free rates in the data, the fact that the volatility of our model-implied risk-free rates also coincides with the data moment provides additional support for our benchmark rational learning model.

The contrast between the adaptive learning model and the rational learning model in Panel II in Table 2 shows that the finding of Cogley and Sargent (2008) does not hold in the context of our asset pricing model. Cogley and Sargent find that using the exact Bayesian approach yields similar asset pricing results as using the anticipated utility framework based on Kreps (1998) that neglects parameter uncertainty. However, in their conclusion, they anticipate our finding by acknowledging that "anticipated-utility modeling may be problematic for applications in finance when high risk aversion is assumed." Furthermore, the excellent approximation by the anticipated-utility approach in Cogley and Sargent (2008) is achieved when agents have CRRA utility. When agents have Epstein-Zin preferences, however, we demonstrate that parameter uncertainty can play an important role in asset pricing by showing that the rational learning model and the adaptive learning model yield very different asset returns. The importance of parameter uncertainty in asset pricing under Esptein-Zin preferences is also emphasized by Collin-Dufresne, Johannes, and Lochstoer (2013).

3.2.2 Return predictability

In this subsection, we run predictive regressions of excess equity returns on lagged dividend price ratios using both the data and the model-implied asset prices of the four models:

$$\ln R^e_{t \to t+k} - \ln R^f_{t \to t+k} = \alpha_k + \beta_k \ln (D_t/P_t) + \nu_{t+k}, \quad (3.1)$$

where the left-hand side is the future excess return on equity, k denotes the forecasting horizon, and D_t/P_t is the dividend price ratio. Following the common practice in the literature, we run predictive regressions over horizons ranging from one to five years.

Table 3 reports the slope coefficients β_k and R^2 from the regressions. The regression results from the data shown in Panel I confirm the findings in the literature that the dividend price ratio has significant predictive power over future excess returns. Moreover, both the estimate of β_k and the value of R^2 increase with the forecasting horizon.

The results from the four models are shown in Panel II of Table 3. The dividend-price ratio has no predictive power in the model with no learning since the ratio is constant in the absence of disaster realizations. The dividend-price ratio in the state learning model exhibits some predictive power, with marginally significant β_k and rather low R^2. Both the rational learning (benchmark) model and the adaptive learning model have positive and significant β_k at each forecasting horizon, although the values of β_k are higher than their data counterparts. Moreover, β_k in these two models increases with the forecasting horizon – a pattern that is consistent with the data. These results confirm the finding of Timmermann (1996) and Timmermann (2001) that the learning effect on stock price dynamics is an intuitive candidate for explaining the predictability of excess returns. Timmermann (1996) offers an intuitive explanation for this finding:

> "An estimated dividend growth rate which is above its true value implies a low dividend yield as investors use a large mark-up factor to form stock prices. Then future returns will tend to be low since the current yield is low and because the estimated growth rate of dividends can be expected to decline to its true value, leading to lower than expected

Table 3: Excess return predictive regressions

Forecasting horizon k		1	2	3	4	5
				Panel I: Data		
U.S. data from 1948 to 2008	β	0.10***	0.18***	0.24***	0.29***	0.38***
	R^2	0.08	0.12	0.16	0.19	0.23
				Panel II: Models		
1. No learning	β	0.00	0.00	0.00	-0.01	0.00
	R^2	0.00	0.00	0.00	0.00	0.00
2. State learning	β	0.73	1.08	1.26	1.35	1.42
	R^2	0.03	0.05	0.05	0.05	0.05
3. Rational learning (benchmark)	β	0.75***	1.06***	1.23***	1.33***	1.39***
	R^2	0.18	0.21	0.21	0.29	0.18
4. Adaptive learning	β	0.78***	0.91***	0.98***	1.03***	1.07***
	R^2	0.28	0.29	0.29	0.29	0.28

* significant at the 90% level, ** 95% level, *** 99% level.

capital gains along the adjustment path." (p.524)

Hence, the predictive power of the dividend-price ratio stems from equity prices reacting more strongly to changes in dividend growth as a result of agents' learning. Consistent with this view and shown in Table 3, the R^2 values for adaptive agents are higher than those for rational agents since equity prices are more responsive to changes in dividend growth for adaptive agents. Relative to the data, the R^2 values in the adaptive learning model are too high at all horizons, whereas the R^2 values in our rational learning (benchmark) model are closer to what the data suggest. None of the models can reproduce the pattern in the data that the predictive power measured by the R^2 value monotonically increases with the forecasting horizon.

4 Conclusion

In this paper, we include learning in a rare disaster model and study its implications on asset prices in an endowment economy. We demonstrate that learning about rare disasters has important implications for asset pricing. When agents are Bayesian learners and face both the uncertainty of whether or not there is a disaster and the uncertainty of the long-term effect of a potential disaster, the asset pricing implications of the model are closer to the data than those of a model without learning. In particular, we do not need to rely on the occurrence of disasters or exogenous variations in disaster probability to generate sizable volatility in stock returns, a great improvement over the existing literature on rare disasters.

In our benchmark model, only aggregate consumption is observable by agents. Adding other observable variables such as investment, output, etc., is likely to further improve our model's performance in matching asset pricing facts because agents' beliefs about future consumption will be more volatile.

In modeling the consumption process, we abstract from the short-term effect of a disaster and focus only on its long-term effect. However, empirical evidence in Nakamura, Steinsson, Barro, and Ursua (2013) shows that the short-term damage of a disaster is on average twice as large as its long-term damage. Extending the current model by incorporating the short-term effect of a disaster could be interesting since not only will asset prices be more responsive to changes in agents' beliefs, agents' beliefs could also be more volatile when the persistence of a disaster shock is closer to that of a normal-time shock. We leave this extension for future research.

References

ABEL, A. B. (1999): "Risk Premia and Term Premia in General Equilibrium," *Journal of Monetary Economics*, 43(1), 3–33.

BACKUS, D. K., M. CHERNOV, AND I. MARTIN (forthcoming): "Disasters Implied by Equity Index Options," *Journal of Finance*.

BANSAL, R., AND A. YARON (2004): "Risks for the Long Run: A Potential Resolution of Asset Pricing Puzzles," *Journal of Finance*, 59(4), 1481 – 1509.

BARRO, R. J. (2006): "Rare Disasters and Asset Markets in the Twentieth Century," *Quarterly Journal of Economics*, 121, 823–866.

BARRO, R. J., AND J. F. URSUA (2009): "Stock Market Crashes and Depressions," *NBER Working Paper 14760*.

BATES, D. (2009): "U.S. Stock Market Crash Risk, 1926 - 2006," *Working Paper University of Iowa*.

BOLLERSLEV, T., AND V. TODOROV (2011): "Tails, Fears, and Risk Premia," *Journal of Finance*, 66(6), 2165–2211.

BRANDT, M., Q. ZENG, AND L. ZHANG (2004): "Equilibrium Stock Return Dynamics under Alternative Rules of Learning about Hidden States," *Journal of Economic Dynamics and Control*, 28(10), 1925–1954.

CAMPBELL, J. Y., AND J. H. COCHRANE (1999): "By Force of Habit: A Consumption-Based Explanation of Aggregate Stock Market Behavior," *Journal of Political Economy*, 107(2), 205–251.

CHEN, H., AND M. PAKOS (2007): "Rational Overreaction and Underreaction in Fixed Income and Equity Markets: The Role of Time-Varying Timing Premium," *GSIA Working Papers*.

COGLEY, T., AND T. J. SARGENT (2008): "Anticipated Utility and Rational Expectations as Approximations of Bayesian Decision Making," *International Economic Review*, 49(1), 185–221.

COLLIN-DUFRESNE, P., M. JOHANNES, AND L. LOCHSTOER (2013): "Parameter Learning in General Equilibrium: The Asset Pricing Implications," *Working Paper Columbia University*.

CONSTANTINIDES, G. M. (2008): "Comment on Barro and Ursua," *Brookings Papers on Economic Activity*.

EPSTEIN, L. G., AND S. ZIN (1989): "Substitution, Risk Aversion and the Temporal Behavior of Consumption and Asset Returns: A Theoretical Framework," *Econometrica*, 57, 937–969.

FARHI, E., S. P. FRAIBERGER, X. GABAIX, R. RANCIERE, AND A. VERDELHAN (2009): "Crash Risk in Currency Markets," *Working Paper*.

FARHI, E., AND X. GABAIX (2008): "Rare Disasters and Exchange Rates," *NBER Working Paper 13805*.

GABAIX, X. (2012): "Variable Rare Disasters: An Exactly Solved Framework for Ten Puzzles in Macro-Finance," *The Quarterly Journal of Economics*, 127(2), 645–700.

GHOSH, A., AND G. M. CONSTANTINIDES (2010): "The Predictability of Returns with Regime Shifts in Consumption and Dividend Growth," *NBER Working Paper 16183*.

GOURIO, F. (2008a): "Disasters and Recoveries," *American Economic Review, Papers and Proceedings*, 98(2), 68–73.

——— (2008b): "Time Series Predictability in the Disaster Model," *Finance Research Letters*, 5(4), 191–203.

——— (2012): "Disaster Risk and Business Cycles," *American Economic Review*, 102(6), 2734–66.

GOURIO, F., M. SIEMER, AND A. VERDELHAN (2013): "International Risk Cycles," *Journal of International Economics*, 89(2), 471–484.

GUO, K. (2009): "Exchange Rates and Asset Prices in An Open Economy with Rare Disasters," *Working Paper*.

JOHANNES, M., L. LOCHSTOER, AND Y. MOU (forthcoming): "Learning about Consumption Dynamics," *Journal of Finance*.

JU, N., AND J. MIAO (2012): "Ambiguity, Learning, and Asset Returns," *Econometrica*, 80(2), 559–591.

JULLIARD, C., AND A. GHOSH (2012): "Can Rare Events Explain the Equity Premium Puzzle?," *Review of Financial Studies*, 25(10), 3037–3076.

KASA, K., AND I.-K. CHO (2011): "Learning and Model Validation," *Society for Economic Dynamics 2011 Meeting Papers*, (1086).

KREPS, D. M. (1998): "Anticipated Utility and Dynamic Choice," *Econometric Society Monographs*, 29, 242–274.

LEWIS, K. (1989): "Can Learning Affect Exchange-Rate Behavior?: The Case of the Dollar in the early 1980's," *Journal of Monetary Economics*, 23(1), 79–100.

LIU, J., J. PAN, AND T. WANG (2005): "An Equilibrium Model of Rare-Event Premia and Its Implication for Option Smirks," *Review of Financial Studies*, 18, 131–164.

MEHRA, R., AND E. PRESCOTT (1985): "The Equity Premium: A Puzzle," *Journal of Monetary Economics*, 15(2), 145–161.

NAKAMURA, E., J. STEINSSON, R. J. BARRO, AND J. F. URSUA (2013): "Crises and Recoveries in an Empirical Model of Consumption Disasters," *American Economic Journal: Macroeconomics*, 5(3), 35–74.

PIAZZESI, M., AND M. SCHNEIDER (2010): "Trend and Cycle in Bond Risk Premia," *Working Paper Stanford University*.

RIETZ, T. A. (1988): "The Equity Risk Premium: A Solution," *Journal of Monetary Economics*, 22, 117–131.

SANTA-CLARA, P., AND S. YAN (2010): "Crashes, Volatility, and the Equity Premium: Lessons from S&P500 Options," *The Review of Economics and Statistics*, 92(2), 435–451.

TIMMERMANN, A. (1996): "Excess Volatility and Predictability of Stock Prices in Autoregressive Dividend Models with Learning," *The Review of Economic Studies*, 63(4), 523–557.

TIMMERMANN, A. (2001): "Structural Breaks, Incomplete Information, and Stock Prices," *Journal of Business & Economic Statistics*, 19(3), 299–314.

VERONESI, P. (1999): "Stock Market Overreactions to Bad News in Good Times: A Rational Expectations Equilibrium Model," *Review of Financial Studies*, 12(5), 975–1007.

——— (2004): "The Peso Problem Hypothesis and Stock Market Returns," *Journal of Economic Dynamics and Control*, 28(4), 707–725.

WACHTER, J. A. (2013): "Can Time-Varying Risk of Rare Disasters Explain Aggregate Stock Market Volatility?," *Journal of Finance*, 68(3), 987–1035.

WEITZMAN, M. (2007): "Subjective Expectations and Asset-Return Puzzles," *The American Economic Review*, 97(4), 1102–1130.

Appendix

A Robustness

This section presents robustness checks for asset pricing moments and predictive regressions.

A.1 Asset pricing moments

Table 4: Robustness - asset pricing moments

	$E(R_f)$	$\sigma(R_f)$	$E(R^e_{lev})$	$\sigma(R^e_{lev})$	$E(R^e_{lev}) - E(R_f)$
Rational learning (benchmark)	1.25	2.17	9.29	17.31	8.05
Larger size of the test	1.36	1.47	8.57	16.32	7.21
Smaller size of the test	0.82	3.47	9.65	19.84	8.83
High risk aversion	0.23	3.18	10.91	18.20	10.67
Low risk aversion	2.31	1.10	7.27	16.01	4.96
High leverage ratio	1.25	2.17	10.32	18.41	9.06
Low leverage ratio	1.25	2.17	8.01	16.16	6.82

Table 4 shows the results of robustness checks on asset pricing moments. The results from the benchmark rational learning model are shown as a reference. We first examine how the size of the test used in setting the learning trigger affects asset pricing moments. Recall that in the benchmark model, the size of the test, α, is 10%. We change the size to $\alpha = 12.5\%$ and $\alpha = 7\%$, respectively, in the case of "Larger size of the test" and the case of "Smaller size of the test". The results show that an increase in the size of the test implies a rise in the risk-free rate, a decline in equity return, and a reduction in return volatility for both risk-free rates and equity returns. An increase in the size of the test means that agents are more likely to falsely reject the null hypothesis ($H_0 : I_t = 1$). Consequently, agents learn less frequently, which mitigates the effects of learning on asset returns. Given that $\alpha = 10\%$ is commonly chosen as the upper bound of a test size in statistical tests, having a smaller size of the test in our benchmark rational learning model could only improve the model's performance in matching data moments.

We next consider an increase (decrease) in the relative risk aversion from $\gamma = 6.5$ to $\gamma = 7.5$ ($\gamma = 5.5$). Intuitively, an increase (decrease) in risk aversion makes asset prices more (less) responsive to changes in agents' beliefs. As a result, both the equity premium and the equity return volatility increase (decrease).

Finally, we consider the cases of a higher leverage ratio ($\lambda = 3$) and a lower leverage ratio ($\lambda = 2$) than the leverage ratio in the main text ($\lambda = 2.5$). Because a change in leverage ratio only affects levered equity returns, the risk-free rates remain unchanged. An increase in leverage ratio amplifies the effect of consumption shocks on equity prices, therefore resulting in a higher equity return, a higher equity premium and a higher equity return volatility.

Although the results are found sensitive to both the relative risk aversion γ and the leverage ratio λ, the values of γ and λ in the calibration of the main text are both set at conservative levels ($\gamma = 6.5$ and $\lambda = 2.5$) by the standard of the literature. It shows that with the help of rational learning, our simple benchmark model can match the data moments using reasonable parameter values, even in the absence of disaster realizations.

A.2 Predictive regressions

Let us now turn to the predictive regressions. Table 5 shows that the basic patterns of the results from our benchmark rational learning model do not change significantly in the robustness checks: the estimates for β_k are all positive and significant; the β_k value increases with the forecasting horizon, and the R^2 value follows an inverse u-shaped pattern with respect to the forecasting horizon.

Table 5: Robustness – excess return predictive regressions

Forecasting horizon k		1	2	3	4	5
Rational learning (benchmark)	β	0.75***	1.06***	1.23***	1.33***	1.39***
	R^2	0.18	0.21	0.21	0.29	0.18
High Learning Threshold	β	0.78***	1.09***	1.24***	1.34***	1.39***
	R^2	0.13	0.15	0.14	0.14	0.13
Low Learning Threshold	β	0.73***	1.04***	1.20***	1.30***	1.36***
	R^2	0.25	0.30	0.30	0.29	0.28
High Risk Aversion	β	0.82***	1.17***	1.35***	1.45***	1.51***
	R^2	0.24	0.28	0.27	0.26	0.24
Low Risk Aversion	β	0.69***	0.96***	1.11***	1.20***	1.26***
	R^2	0.11	0.12	0.12	0.12	0.11
High Leverage	β	0.73***	1.03***	1.20***	1.29***	1.35***
	R^2	020	0.23	0.23	0.22	0.21
Low Leverage	β	0.80***	1.13***	1.31***	1.41***	1.47***
	R^2	0.15	0.18	0.17	0.16	0.15

* significant at the 90% level, ** 95% level, *** 99% level.